Central Bank Independence: What Is It and What Will It Do For Us?

GEOFFREY E. WOOD
City University Business School

TERENCE C. MILLS
University of Hull

FORREST H. CAPIE
City University Business School

Institute of Economic Affairs
1993

First published in January 1993
by
THE INSTITUTE OF ECONOMIC AFFAIRS
2 Lord North Street, Westminster, London SW1P 3LB

© The Institute of Economic Affairs 1993

Current Controversies No. 4

All rights reserved

ISBN 0-255 36315-X

The Institute gratefully acknowledges financial support for its publications programme and other work from a generous benefaction by the late Alec and Beryl Warren.

All the Institute's publications seek to further its objective of promoting the advancement of learning, by research into economic and political science, by education of the public therein, and by the dissemination of ideas, research and the results of research in these subjects. The views expressed are those of the authors, not of the IEA, which has no corporate view.

Printed in Great Britain by
GORON PRO-PRINT CO LTD, LANCING, WEST SUSSEX
Set in Berthold Bembo 11 on 13 point

Contents

FOREWORD	*Colin Robinson*	5
THE AUTHORS		7
Introduction		9
1. The Meaning of Independence		10
2. Why Independence?		11
Researching the Facts of Central Bank Performance		12
A Major Problem		13
3. The Data and its Analysis		14
The Gold Standard and Other Animals		15
US Experience: Mono or Bimetallism?		16
Summary of Countries' Experience		17
An Exploratory Classification		17
4. Conclusions		22
Why Not Zero Inflation?		26
'Independence' of NZ Type Would Help		27
Statistical Annex		28
REFERENCES		31
FIGURES		
1. Inflation Scatterplot		19
2. Inflation Scatterplot: Pre-1914		20
3. Inflation Scatterplot: Inter-War		21

4.	Inflation Scatterplot: 1947-1971	22
5.	Inflation Scatterplot: 1972-1988	23
6.	Smoothed Inflation: UK and Germany, 1870-1988	24
7.	Smoothed Inflation: Canada and New Zealand, 1911-1988 (Canada), and 1915-1988 (New Zealand)	25
8.	'Mean-Standard Deviation' Scatterplot	29

TABLE

1.	Central Bank Classifications	18

Foreword

THE POOR PERFORMANCE of the British economy in the last few years has resulted in increased questioning of the rôles, the structures and the inter-relationships of the institutions which have traditionally made macro-economic policy. There is also a perceived need for more open policy-making. The Chancellor has responded by instituting a monthly monetary report from the Treasury and the Bank of England and by appointing seven economists who will advise on economic forecasts and economic policy generally.

High on many people's lists of reforms is independence for the Bank of England. Indeed, in the first publication in the *Current Controversies* series, Professor Gordon Pepper argued in favour of such independence.[1]

But what does 'independence' mean? And what does the empirical evidence suggest about whether differences between countries in terms of central bank dependence are reflected in differences in inflation performance? The Bundesbank appears to have delivered a low rate of inflation but is that because of its relationship to government or is it because of other features of the German economy and of German society?

In Current Controversies No. 4, Professors Wood, Mills and Capie discuss the concept of independence, survey existing evidence about the relationship between independence and inflation, and set out some empirical work of their own, based on both cross-sections and time-series, which covers a long period of data.

Even though they describe the data analysis as 'exploratory', the authors produce evidence that independence is sufficient for low (though not zero) inflation. Nevertheless, independence is evidently not a necessary condition: some countries with 'dependent' central banks, such as Sweden, also have low inflation.

---

[1] Gordon Pepper, *Restoring Credibility: Monetary Policy Now*, Current Controversies No. 1, London: Institute of Economic Affairs, October 1992.

As regards independence for the Bank of England, the paper concludes that

> '... when, as now, the change in central bank status would be made against a background of unsatisfactory monetary performance, granting a central bank independence will help to lower inflation'. (p. 27)

Moreover, the authors can see a model in the Reserve Bank of New Zealand whose position is unusual in that it is given a clear mandate by government – at present to reduce inflation to 0-2 per cent by end-1993. They argue the case for giving the central bank a clear mandate and only one objective, and they reach the interesting conclusion that

> 'Just as the Bank of England provided a model when the Reserve Bank of New Zealand was established in 1934, there is now a clear case for making the Reserve Bank of New Zealand a model for a reformed Bank of England.' (p. 27)

As in all IEA papers, the views expressed in Current Controversies No. 4 are those of the authors, not those of the Institute (which has no corporate view), its Trustees, Directors or Advisers. It is published as a contribution to public debate about the topical issue of central bank independence.

January 1993   COLIN ROBINSON
*Editorial Director,
Institute of Economic Affairs*

The Authors

GEOFFREY E. WOOD is Professor of Economics at the City University Business School. He has taught at Warwick University and been on the research staff of both the Bank of England and the Federal Reserve Bank of St. Louis. He is co-author of *Financing Procedures in British Foreign Trade* (1980), and co-editor of, among others, *Monetary Targets* (1980), *Financial Crises and the World Banking System* (1985), and *Macro-Economic Policy and Economic Interdependence* (1989). He is Economic Adviser to The Union Discount Company of London.

Professor Wood has been a member of the IEA's Advisory Council since 1987, and has recently (1991) been made a Trustee. For the IEA he has written (with Gordon Pepper) *Too Much Money...?* (Hobart Paper No. 68, 1976), and has contributed to other IEA Papers, including a Commentary in *The State of Taxation* (IEA Readings No. 16, 1977), and papers in *Could Do Better* (Occasional Paper No. 62, 1982), *Agenda for Social Democracy* (Hobart Paperback No. 15, 1983), and *Whose Europe?* (IEA Readings No. 29, 1989); he contributed a new Introduction to the Third Edition of F. A. Hayek's *Denationalisation of Money* (Hobart Paper No. 70, 1990); and he wrote the Introduction to *The State of the Economy 1991* (IEA Readings No. 34, 1991).

TERENCE C. MILLS is currently Professor of Applied Economics and Dean of the School of Economic Studies at the University of Hull. He is a graduate of the universities of Essex and Warwick, where his PhD thesis investigated the econometric relationships between money, output, prices and interest rates in the UK. From 1976 to 1988 he was Lecturer in Econometrics at the University of Leeds, and between 1980 and 1984 he was also attached to the Monetary Policy Group at the Bank of England. Between 1988 and 1990 he was successively Senior, then Professorial, Research Fellow at the Centre for Financial Markets, City University Business School.

He is author of *Time Series Techniques for Economists*, published in 1990 by Cambridge University Press, who are also publishing his latest book, *The Econometric Modelling of Financial Time Series*, in 1993. He is the author of some 60 articles in journals and edited books, primarily on applying time-series techniques to issues in macro-economics, monetary economics, economic history and financial markets. For the IEA he has previously written *Predicting the Unpredictable?* (Occasional Paper No. 87, 1992).

FORREST H. CAPIE is Professor of Economic History at the City University Business School, London. He holds a PhD from the LSE, and has taught at the universities of Warwick and Leeds. He was British Academy Overseas Visiting Fellow at the National Bureau of Economic Research, New York, in 1978, and Visitor at the University of Aix-Marseille in 1979. He has written extensively on economic history in the 19th and 20th centuries. Recent books of which he is the author and/or editor include: *Depression and Protectionism* (1983); *A Monetary History of the United Kingdom, 1870-1982* (1985); *Major Inflations in History* (1991); and *Unregulated Banking: Chaos or Order?* (1991). For the IEA he has written *Have the Banks Failed British Industry?* (jointly with Michael Collins) (Hobart Paper No. 119, July 1992), and *Trade Wars: A Repetition of the Inter-War Years?* (Current Controversies No. 2, December 1992).

Central Bank Independence: What Is It and What Will It Do For Us?

GEOFFREY E. WOOD, TERENCE C. MILLS AND FORREST H. CAPIE

Introduction

THERE HAS BEEN a surge of interest in the process by which monetary policy decisions are made in the UK. In particular, attention has been focussed on the relationship between the Bank of England and the Treasury. Several authors have urged that the Bank should be made 'independent' – that is, that it should have sole responsibility for, and decision-making power over, the conduct of monetary policy. Such advice is readily understandable, for there is close at hand a telling example of the benefits that apparently flow from such 'independence'. The German central bank, the Bundesbank, is 'independent': although its relationship with the German government is complex, the term is a useful shorthand. The German price level has risen by approximately 200 per cent since 1950, while in the UK prices have risen by about 1,200 per cent over the same period.

A large body of academic research – both theoretical and empirical – suggests that central bank independence will bring, and indeed is necessary for, low inflation: all in all, the results of that research seem compelling. It does, however, leave some questions. Before carrying out a major institutional change, as changing the status of the Bank of England would surely be, it is desirable to have unanswered as few questions bearing on it as possible.

The aim of this paper is to address some of those questions. Section 1 discusses what is meant by 'independence'. We then review the main strands of theoretical and empirical work which have suggested that 'independence' is desirable. That leads us to highlight some questions raised by that work, and to provide our answers to some of those questions. In the concluding section, we draw out policy conclusions from our results. There is a brief annex for those interested in the details of the statistical methods we have employed.

1. The Meaning of Independence

MOST RECENT WORK on the connection between central bank-government relations and inflation proceeds on the basis that the meaning of 'independence' is obvious. The implicit assumption is that it means simply that the government of the day has no formal means of influencing central bank decisions over monetary policy. Ways in which such formal influence might be exerted are then examined, and banks ranked in independence according to the number of such channels; examples of such work are discussed in detail in Section 2 (below, pp. 12-13).

One study has, however, considered what independence can mean – an essay by Milton Friedman, first published in 1962[1] (reprinted in 1968: page references are to the reprint). The starting point of his discussion was the question: '... [W]hat kind of arrangements should a free society set up for the control of monetary policy?'[2] Control over money, to quote Friedman again, is 'a potent tool for controlling and shaping the economy'.[3] How can power be dispersed, as it should be to preserve freedom, in control over money? According to Friedman:

> 'The problem is to establish institutional arrangements that will enable government to exercise responsibility for money, yet will at the same time limit the power given to government and prevent the power from being used in ways that will tend to weaken rather than strengthen a free society.'[4]

It was in the context of addressing that problem that Friedman considered the concept of independence. He examined in turn an automatic commodity standard such as the gold standard, central bank independence, and finally legislative rules governing money growth. There is, he suggested, a 'trivial meaning' of the word

[1] Friedman (1962).
[2] Friedman (1968, p. 173).
[3] Friedman (1968, p. 174).
[4] Friedman (1968, p. 174).

'independence' – when, within an agency of government, monetary policy is entrusted to some separate organisation which is subject to the head of that agency. In that sense, the Bank of England is at present independent.

Friedman then goes on to suggest 'a more basic meaning', which is that the central bank should be 'an independent branch of government, co-ordinate with the legislative, executive and judicial branches'.[1] It would, that is to say, have a mandate, analogous to the mandate given to the judiciary. It would carry out a law or laws passed by the government, and its operations could be interfered with by government only if the law – its mandate – were changed. Friedman goes on to suggest several grounds for doubting the efficacy of such a proposal, and to argue that a monetary rule is likely to be more effective. We do not pursue that discussion here. What is important to note is that few central banks actually have a specific mandate. The Reserve Bank of New Zealand, with a clear mandate to deliver 0-2 per cent inflation, is apparently unique. When central banks have explicit mandates (and not all do), they are usually imprecise and often specify multiple objectives – the Bundesbank's mandate exemplifies both characteristics.

We turn again to this question of the meaning of independence and to the nature of the central bank's mandate after we have set out the results of our empirical work.

2. Why Independence?

SEVERAL SCHOLARS have constructed analytical models which predict that when run by government, monetary policy will produce too high inflation.[2] The argument in outline is fairly straightforward. Monetary policy affects the general price level. Unexpected increases in the price level (but not expected ones) temporarily expand economic activity, and unexpected declines in the price level reduce activity – i.e., there is a 'short-run Phillips curve'. Voters value expansions of output, but they dislike inflation.

In such a setting, the government has a motive to increase

[1] Friedman (1968, p. 179).
[2] Barro and Gordon (1983) is perhaps the best-known example.

inflation so as to stimulate output. But voters know that, and therefore expect inflation. Hence the policy-maker must supply inflation *to prevent a temporary squeeze on output*. Since the inflation is expected, it brings no output benefits, but it does bring the costs of inflation.

This can be prevented by one of two routes. The policy-maker can commit himself not to inflate. If this is believed, then inflation is not expected and he is under no pressure to inflate so as to prevent a fall in output. Alternatively, monetary policy can be removed from the hands of politicians and given to a body which has no incentive to try and win favour with the electorate – i.e., to an independent central bank.[1]

Researching the Facts of Central Bank Performance

So much for the theory. What about the facts? The earliest examination was a paper by Robin Bade and Michael Parkin in 1978. It is better known, however, in its revised and expanded 1987 version, in which they examine 12 countries during the years 1973 to 1986.[2] (Most studies start in 1973 or later; the reasons for this are discussed below, pp. 13-14.)

Bade and Parkin distinguish two types of government influence on central banks, calling them the 'financial type' and the 'policy type'. 'Financial type' concerns government influence in selecting board members; in setting their salaries; in determining the bank's budget; and in determining who gets the profits. 'Policy type' refers to government influence in board meetings, and whether government has the final say on monetary policy. Bade and Parkin found that 'policy type' influence was crucial: central banks free of it delivered significantly lower inflation than did those susceptible to such influence.

Another approach to the measurement of independence was

---

[1] Barro and Gordon (and several other authors) have considered whether reputation can be substituted for a formal rule. Does the custom of delivering price stability lead that behaviour to be expected, so that there is no need to inflate to prevent a rise in unemployment? The answer, from a somewhat complex and mathematical literature, is that it may, but need not, lead to that desired result. The most accessible, although still not easy, review of this discussion can be found in Grossman (1991).

[2] Bade and Parkin (1987).

that by Masciandero and Tabellini.[1] In their study of five Pacific basin countries (Australia, Canada, Japan, New Zealand and the USA), they focussed attention on government influence on the appointment of the board and subsequently on the board's decisions. Their primary concern was with the relationship between central bank dependency and fiscal deficits, but that between dependency and inflation was also examined. The conclusion supported Bade and Parkin, as did related work by Alesina.[2] All in all, the empirical work displays what may be seen as a remarkable consensus.

A Major Problem

Nevertheless, before accepting the conclusion, it should be recognised that there is a major empirical problem with these studies: they all cover overlapping time-periods and, in some cases, partially overlapping sets of countries. Of course, this does not mean that their conclusion is wrong, but it does open the possibility that they have found a result unique to that particular set of data. As Friedman and Schwartz (1991) point out, such an event is not unknown, and it is important to test an hypothesis on data sets other than those which suggested the hypothesis.[3]

Of course, these earlier authors had a good reason for not using data from before 1973. That was the year in which Bretton Woods, the world-wide system of pegged exchange rates established after the Second World War, broke down.

In such a pegged exchange rate system, the monetary policies of each country are linked by the commitment to keep exchange rates unchanged. The ERM, and British monetary policy since Britain's departure from the ERM, illustrate this well. All the countries which have remained in the ERM have similar interest rates and all also have very similar rates of inflation. Britain, in contrast, has moved its interest rates significantly away from those of the remaining ERM members.

---

[1] Masciandero and Tabellini (1988).

[2] See Alesina (1988, 1989) and Alesina and Summers (1991).

[3] Friedman provides a telling and amusing example of this drawn from his own experience as a statistician in US government service during the Second World War: see the appendix to Friedman and Schwartz (1991).

The classic exposition of why fixed exchange rates lock monetary policies together was provided by David Hume in 1754.[1] In summary, if one country were to inflate faster than another and the exchange rate did not change, the demand for goods would be diverted from the high- to the low-inflation country; money would flow in the same direction, so as to buy the goods; and inflation would fall in the high-inflation country and rise in the low-inflation one.[2]

Accordingly, if all countries in a pegged exchange rate system are compelled to have the same rate of inflation, then, whatever the influences on that rate, the status of national central banks cannot be among them. That argument is, however, pushed too far when it is used to claim that data prior to 1973 cannot be employed to consider the significance of central bank independence because *fixing* of exchange rates, such as Hume discussed and the above discussion has assumed, was never actually the norm. We describe the various exchange rate régimes before 1973 in the next section of this paper, where we also discuss our data and present some results.

3. The Data and its Analysis

OUR DATA comprise annual rates of inflation for 14 countries, drawn primarily from Mitchell: the earliest starting date is 1871, the latest 1916, with all series ending in 1988.[3]

This period encompasses a variety of exchange rate régimes and a variety of inflationary experiences, including hyper-inflations. These latter episodes, which would, in any case, require detailed

---

[1] Hume (1754), reprinted (e.g. 1987).

[2] Hume's original essay is well worth reading; this brief summary gives no flavour of the felicity of Hume's prose, and only a sketch of his subtle argument.

[3] Mitchell (1981, 1982, 1983). The consumer price index was used and, where this was not available, the cost of living index was employed. Some previous studies, for example Alesina (1989), examine the effects of government influence on inflation and unemployment. Not only do the data not permit examination of these effects over a long run: we are not persuaded that the question is well chosen. It is certainly not produced from the time-consistency framework which motivates the work and, as money is neutral over a long period, we are not sure what the results, if any, would tell us.

within-year inflation data, are not explicitly considered, for they have inevitably resulted from a breakdown of the government's tax-gathering capacity in the face of civil unrest, or in the extreme, civil war or revolution.[1] Examples in the period covered in this paper are Russia after 1917, Hungary in 1919, Poland in the early 1920s, Germany in the same period (when there were attempted communist coups and a Bolshevik government in Bavaria); and, after the Second World War, China and Greece, both with civil war.[2]

In all these cases, resort to the 'inflation tax' was a last desperate gamble, after many other legislative restraints had already been overthrown. They do not, therefore, provide suitable data to test the effects of the niceties of central bank-government relations. Nor do we explore the possible significance of whether countries are industrialised or not. This interesting distinction has been examined by Cukierman; unfortunately, too few non-industrialised countries have the long runs of data we exploit in this paper.[3]

The Gold Standard and Other Animals

What were the exchange rate régimes of this period? Before 1914, not every country was on the Gold Standard and few seemed to regard it as being as immutable as Britain did. For the core countries of the world economy (France, Germany, the USA and the UK), it was essentially a rule which guided monetary policy; for the remainder it was more akin to a pegged exchange rate régime such as that of Bretton Woods.[4]

Adherence to the Gold Standard sometimes proved impossible and, whilst there was considerable success, there were often occasions when the pressures on countries proved too great, particularly in times of war or serious financial crisis. Such indeed was the case with Britain in 1797 when she had to suspend convertibility during the Napoleonic Wars. Although gold convertibility was eventually restored in 1821, it had to be suspended again in 1914. Similar experiences were quite common.

[1] They are, however, discussed in Capie (1986) and Capie and Wood (1991).
[2] There are other episodes from earlier years: see Capie (1986).
[3] See Cukierman (1992).
[4] Further discussion of this can be found in Bernholz (1986).

But even in the heyday of the classical Gold Standard – 1880 to 1913 – there were countries which found it impossible to behave in a way that allowed them to join the Gold Standard or, for those which did manage it, to adhere to the standard. Spain, for example, was in the former category. Without formally joining the standard, but instead staying with bimetallism, Spain behaved as if constrained by gold standard rules. But in 1882 convertibility was suspended and thereafter she made a bold attempt at what today would be called convergence to the path of her European neighbours, although without complete success.

Italy, on the other hand, abandoned convertibility into gold in 1866, and then immediately considered returning but could not: it was 1884 before convertibility was restored. Public finances, however, deteriorated again and in 1894 the standard was abandoned for a second time.

It was in Latin America that there was least success with the standard. In 1883 Argentina formally rejoined the Gold Standard after an absence, only to return to inconvertibility the following year, although in 1890 she once again rejoined. (Argentina also led the way off the new standard in the 1920s, abandoning it in 1929.) Similarly Chile, which had been on gold from 1870, suspended convertibility in 1878 following a financial crisis. She then restored the standard in 1895 at a depreciated parity, abandoning it yet again in 1898.

US Experience: Mono or Bimetallism?

Even where the standard was not abandoned there were instances where it could easily have been. The most notable was the United States, which had been on the Gold Standard *de jure* since 1879 (and *de facto* somewhat longer). But in the 1890s serious consideration was given to restoring the use of silver: indeed, the famous election campaign of 1896 was fought on that issue. There was no guarantee that the USA would adhere to monometallism, as was evidenced by the seriousness with which the issue of bimetallism was taken.

In the inter-war years, international monetary affairs were in some disarray. Exchange rates floated for the first few years after the First World War, until in 1925 Britain went back to a version of the Gold Standard – the Gold Exchange Standard. Other countries followed in 1926 and 1927, but by 1929 the system was already breaking up.[1] Britain finally abandoned gold in 1931, moving to a managed float, and was followed by all other countries in the next few years. The Americans held on until 1933 and the French, together with a dwindling gold bloc, until 1936. Thus there were, for most of the international economy, more years of floating rates between the two world wars than years of fixed rates with, moreover, the period of fixed rates carrying little conviction.

Even in the Bretton Woods system, there was some degree of monetary independence: Britain, for example, went through several cycles of greater monetary ease than was compatible with maintaining the exchange rate, followed by devaluation and a period of stringency.[2]

Summary of Countries' Experience

In summary, then, throughout the period of this study, most countries had some degree of monetary independence. The range of inflation rates across countries should certainly be expected to be different under different exchange rate régimes. But, given the régimes which have existed, there is no reason to expect the range ever to have been zero because there has generally been room for some degree of national independence. It is therefore clearly worthwhile discovering what the historical data suggest.[3]

An Exploratory Classification

The countries investigated are listed in Table 1, along with a classification of the status of their central bank.[4] Ten of the

---

[1] The Governor of the Bank of England considered devaluation in 1927.

[2] See Williamson and Wood (1976).

[3] An additional reason for examining the historical data was suggested by Herschel Grossman (1991), in his remark that the prediction of higher inflation resulting from politically controlled monetary policy should hold in any period, not just in recent years. This is because governments want revenue even when not dependent on a popular mandate, and inflation helps the government's finances.

[4] Argentina and Brazil were also investigated, but their inflation experience is so markedly different from those listed that they have been excluded from the discussion: their experience serves only to reinforce the general conclusions obtained from our reported statistical analysis.

Table 1
Central Bank Classifications

UK	independent up to 1945, then dependent
USA	independent
Austria	dependent
Belgium	unclassified
Canada	established in 1935, dependent up to 1937, independent up to 1959, then dependent
France	dependent
Germany	dependent up to 1946, then independent
Italy	unclassified
Japan	dependent
New Zealand	established in 1933, independent up to 1935, then dependent; then independent from 1989.
Spain	dependent
Sweden	dependent

countries have been classified into periods in which they had independent or dependent central banks (or none was established) while two, Belgium and Italy, have been left unclassified. The method of classification uses the same criteria as Bade and Parkin and Masciandero and Tabellini; in addition, it takes into account the ownership of the bank, and whether it has the sole right to issue notes and coins. The classification shown in Table 1 is, like the rest of this paper, exploratory. It provides part of the framework within which we examine the data; the results of that examination in turn shed light on the classification.

Figure 1 presents a scatterplot of median inflation against our preferred measure of inflation variability.[1] The higher a point on the vertical axis, the higher the rate of inflation: the further a point is to the right the more variable the inflation rate. Two distinct

---

[1] The Statistical Annex provides details of the statistical techniques used and our reasons for using them.

Figure 1:
Inflation Scatterplot

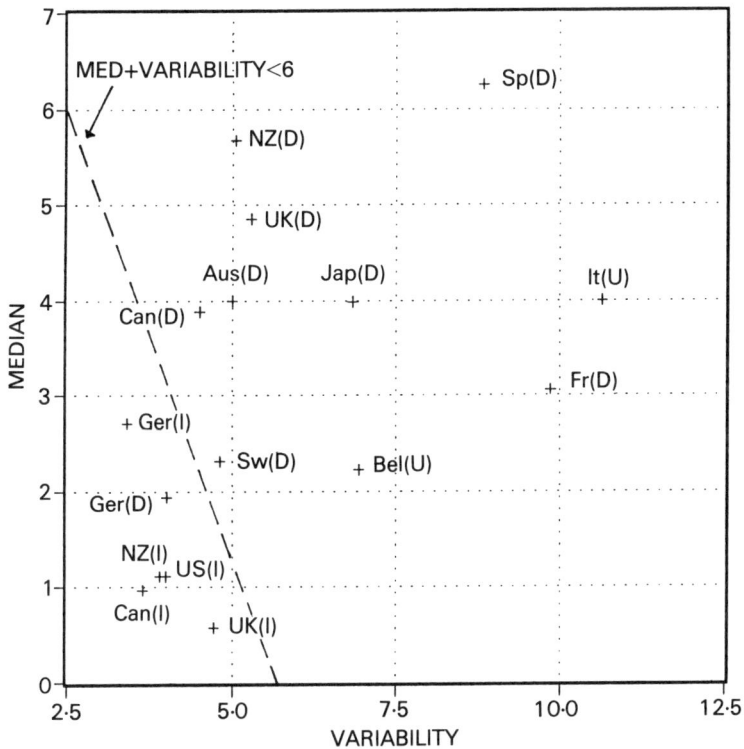

(D): Dependent; (I): Independent; (U): Unclassified

clusters of points are revealed. One contains all the pairs of values calculated using data from periods when countries had independent central banks plus that from the period when Germany had a dependent central bank; the other contains the remaining dependent central bank pairs. Indeed, a simple discriminatory rule is revealed from this scatterplot: if *(median+variability<6)*, the central bank is independent. As a by-product, it appears that, although we had left the Belgian and Italian central banks 'unclassified', such a rule classifies both Belgium and Italy as having dependent central banks.

Figures 2 to 5 (each with different scales) repeat the scatterplots for different time-periods: pre-1914, inter-war, 1947 to 1971 (the

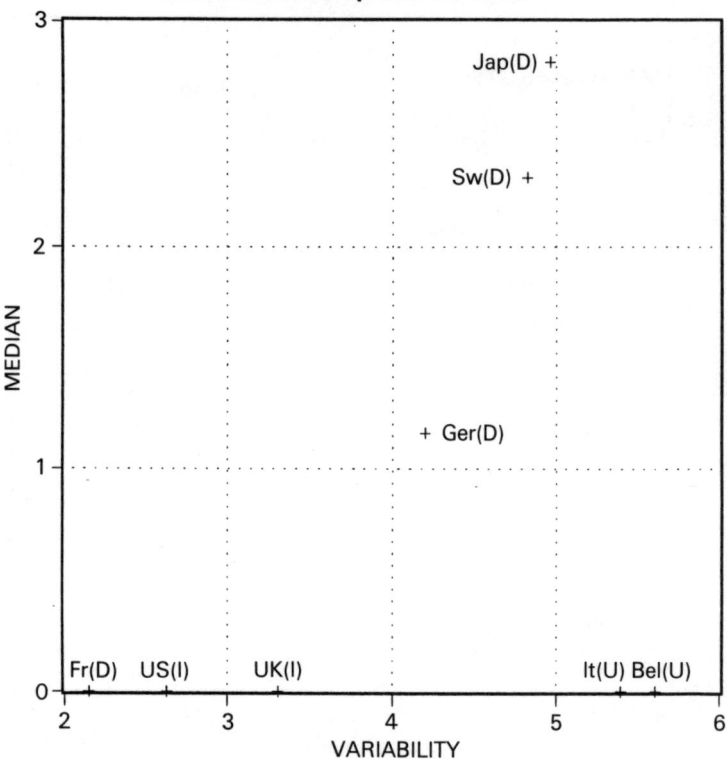

**Figure 2:
Inflation Scatterplot: Pre-1914**

(D): Dependent; (I): Independent; (U): Unclassified

Bretton Woods era), and post-1971. Pre-1914 was a period of low and stable inflation rates, but (France apart) the tendency for countries with dependent central banks to have higher and more variable rates of inflation is readily apparent. During the inter-war period the range of inflation rates was much wider, but again those countries with independent central banks (along with Sweden) experienced lower and more stable rates. The Bretton Woods era shows a marked convergence in inflation experience, although the USA and Germany have the best performance, while the post-Bretton Woods period exhibits the greatest fluctuations in inflation. Nevertheless, the two countries with independent central banks during this last period, the USA and Germany, along

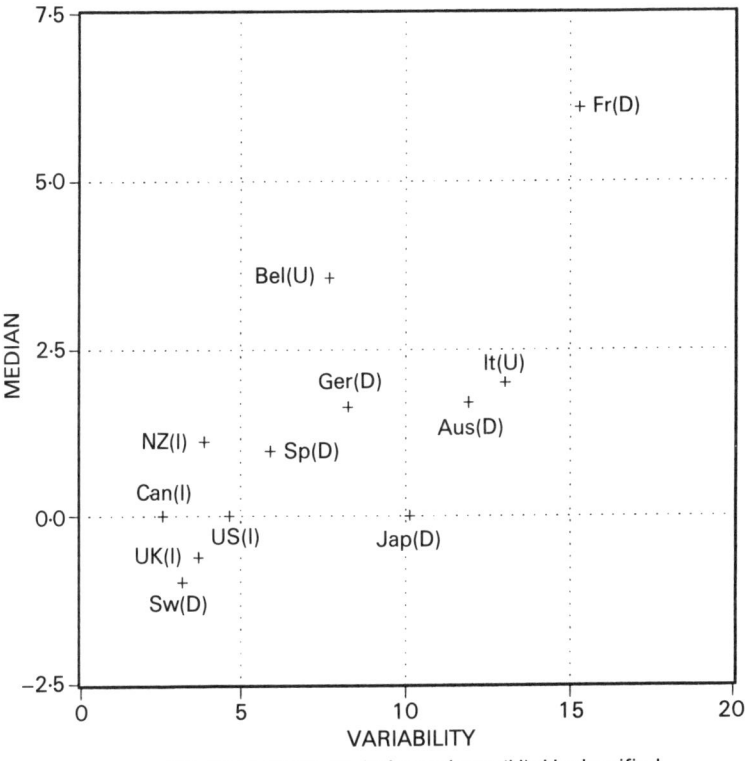

**Figure 3:
Inflation Scatterplot: Inter-War**

(D): Dependent; (I): Independent; (U): Unclassified

with Austria and Belgium, again achieve relatively low and stable inflation.

This analysis has focussed on the 'cross-sectional' inflation performance of central banks, but we can also investigate the inflation behaviour of the countries in our sample individually through time.

Figures 6 and 7 present 'smoothed' inflation rates for those four countries which underwent a 'constitutional change' in their central bank during the sample period (see Table 1): the UK, Germany, Canada and New Zealand. These figures confirm our previous results relating to the move to a dependent central bank in the UK, Canada and New Zealand: apart from the First World

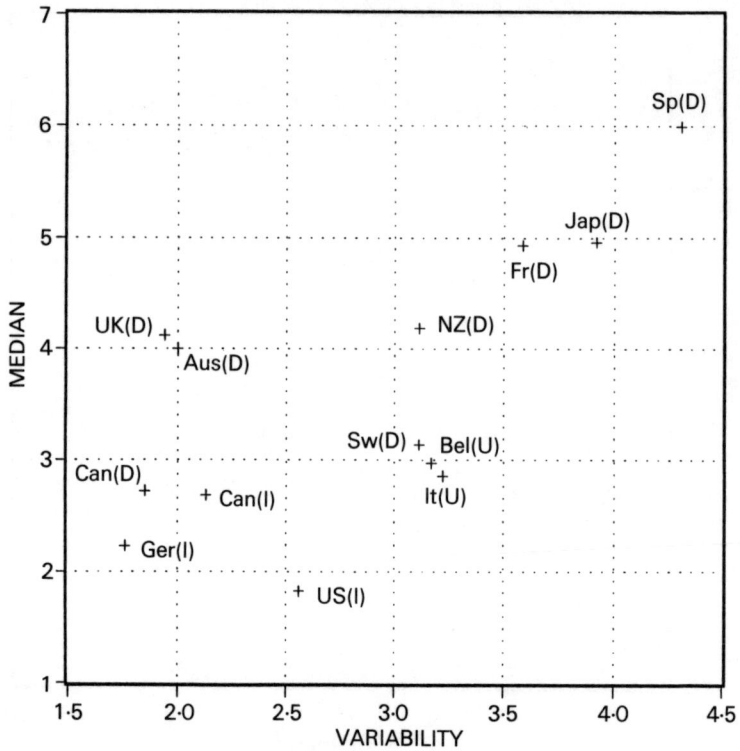

Figure 4:
Inflation Scatterplot: 1947-1971

(D): Dependent; (I): Independent; (U): Unclassified

War, inflation rates have tended to be higher after the move than before it. For Germany, which moved from a dependent to an independent central bank in 1945, inflation behaviour seems to have been rather similar under both régimes, if the period of the early 1920s is ignored: that is also consistent with our previous results.

4. Conclusions

THE RESULTS set out in this paper are certainly consistent with the belief that independent central banks will deliver lower inflation than will dependent banks whether one examines the contrasting

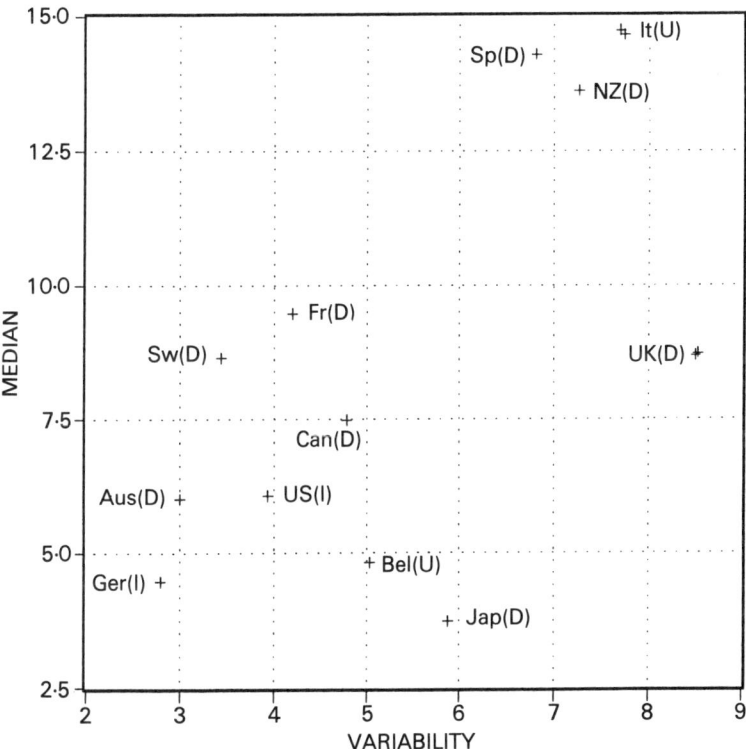

**Figure 5:
Inflation Scatterplot: 1972-1988**

(D): Dependent; (I): Independent; (U): Unclassified

performance of dependent and independent banks in different countries, or the change in behaviour when the status of a central bank is altered.

Nevertheless, the results do not in our view lead directly to the conclusion that granting central banks independence will lower rates of inflation, for two reasons.

○ *First*, because there is clear evidence that while independence may be sufficient for low inflation, it is certainly not necessary – note in evidence of this Sweden and Germany. Sweden's dependent bank performs almost as well as the independents, and (provided we exclude the hyperinflation of the 1920s)

[*Cont'd. on p. 26*]

Figure 6:
Smoothed Inflation: UK and Germany, 1870-1988

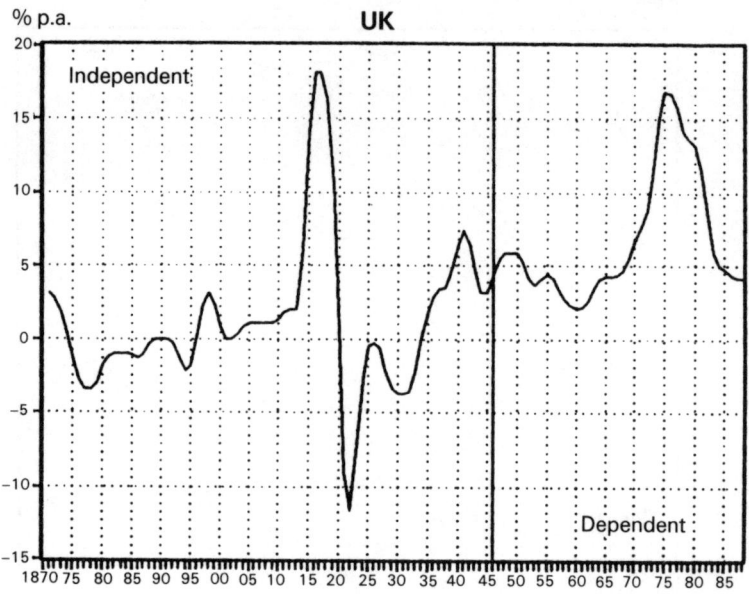

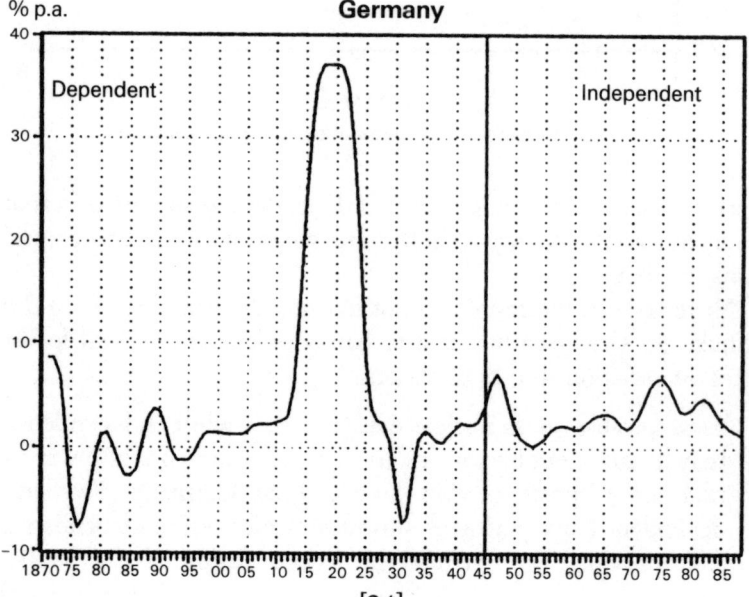

[24]

**Figure 7:
Smoothed Inflation: Canada and New Zealand**

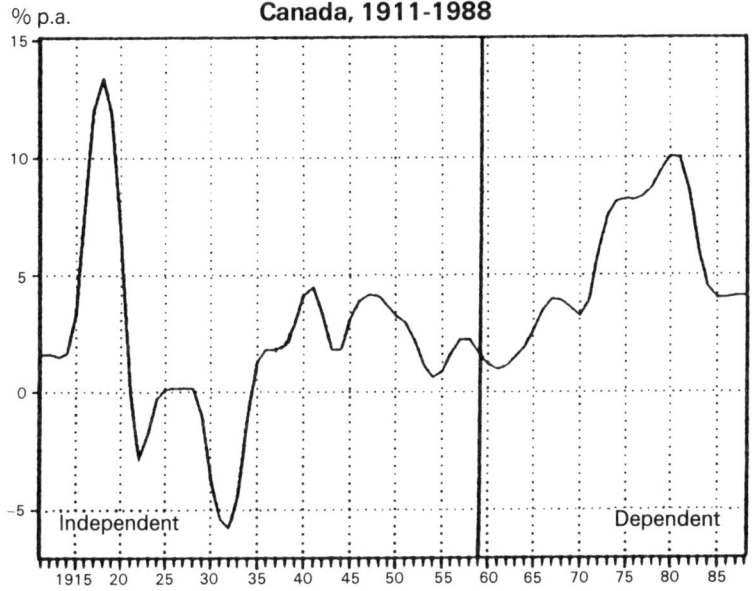

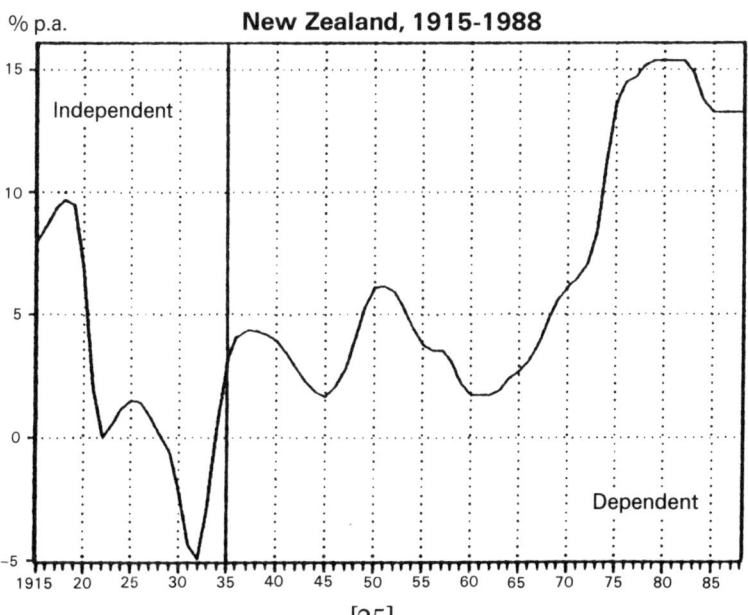

Germany has been a low-inflation country regardless of the status of its central bank.

- *Second*, of the central banks which appear to have similar ambiguous status for similar reasons, Belgium and Italy, one produced relatively low inflation, the other high. These points suggest that something other than independence, for which independence is a good but not perfect proxy, may be important.

It should also be observed that a change in a central bank's status is not, except in the case of Germany after 1945, exogenous to the previous economic history of the country. That history may therefore lie behind the change in performance, or at least contribute to it.

Why Not Zero Inflation?

There are two further problems our paper has not addressed, and which are of considerable importance. First, why do independent central banks deliver low inflation, but not stable prices – not, in other words, zero inflation? If we accept 0-2 per cent inflation as being, in effect, price stability, on the ground that quality improvement is not properly allowed for in most price indices, that is what the theoretical models lead one to predict an independent central bank would deliver. But none does. Why not? Is the independence imperfect, or does the confusion of mandate matter? The latter may be the source of the problem; for the (formerly dependent) Reserve Bank of New Zealand now has a clear mandate for 0-2 per cent inflation, and has achieved it. But that can be no more than a conjecture, for it has not achieved it for long and it is, in any case, only one central bank. A theory cannot be confirmed by just one observation!

Furthermore, why do independent central banks which do not have a clear low-inflation mandate act in the public interest? Why do they not act in their *own* interest, as the burgeoning 'public choice' literature suggests they should? Or do their own and the public interest coincide, for some as yet unknown reason? Although we cannot answer these last two questions, and can offer only a conjecture to the previous one, they are important in considering whether Britain should have an independent central bank.

'Independence' of NZ Type Would Help

Our results suggest that, especially when, as now, the change in central bank status would be made against a background of unsatisfactory monetary performance, granting a central bank independence will help to lower inflation. Making the 'independence' of the type analysed by Milton Friedman, and adopted by New Zealand in 1989, is surely what is desirable. The Reserve Bank of New Zealand was given a clear mandate – to reduce inflation to 0-2 per cent by the end of 1993. That was the only objective assigned to monetary policy, and the bank was solely responsible for that policy. The reform has worked. Inflation in New Zealand is now below 2 per cent and attention is being given to rolling on the target. Giving a clear mandate and only one objective ensures that the central bank acts in the public interest, and also ensures that there is no conflict between the objectives assigned to the central bank.[1]

Just as the Bank of England provided a model when the Reserve Bank of New Zealand was established in 1934, there is now a clear case for making the Reserve Bank of New Zealand a model for a reformed Bank of England. Both the questions we have answered in this paper and those questions we have raised but not answered point to that conclusion.

---

[1] Whether the mandate should be in terms of the ultimate objective of monetary policy, the price level, or in terms of a measure of the money supply, is not considered in this paper. Interesting discussions of the analytical, as opposed to the usually discussed statistical, issues are contained in Barro (1986) and Friedman (1960).

Statistical Annex

When examining the relationship between central bank dependency and the rate of inflation, it is tempting to compute the mean and variance (or the latter's square root, the standard deviation) to provide measures of 'average' inflation and its 'variability'. It is well known, however, that the mean is only appropriate when the distribution of inflation rates is approximately symmetric, while the variance requires the distribution to be approximately normal – i.e., that it is not only symmetric but also 'bell-shaped'. The two statistics are also heavily influenced by the presence of extreme observations ('outliers'). When a distribution is asymmetric and when outliers are present, it is necessary to consider alternative measures of 'average' and 'variability' that are not dependent upon the assumption of normality or even just symmetry: such statistics are called 'robust'.

The use of robust statistics is important in this paper because inflation rates are typical of 'asymmetric' time-series having outliers. A simple yet robust measure of the 'average' is the median, that number for which there are as many values greater than or equal to it as there are values that are smaller than or equal to it. The median is a good measure of 'average' behaviour when the data are skewed and contain outliers, particularly with small sample sizes, as are some of the inflation series considered in this paper.[1]

Our measure of inflation variability is the H-spread, which is the difference between those values which split into half the two halves of the data initially split by the median (and hence are similar to quartiles).[2]

---

[1] Tests of non-normality and skewness are reported in detail in Capie, Mills and Wood (1992), where further discussion of the statistical techniques may be found.

[2] The statistical reasoning underlying this measure is developed in, for example, Mills (1990, Chapter 3), which provides a textbook discussion of these concepts of exploratory data analysis within the context of analysing economic time-series.

Figure 8:
'Mean-Standard Deviation' Scatterplot

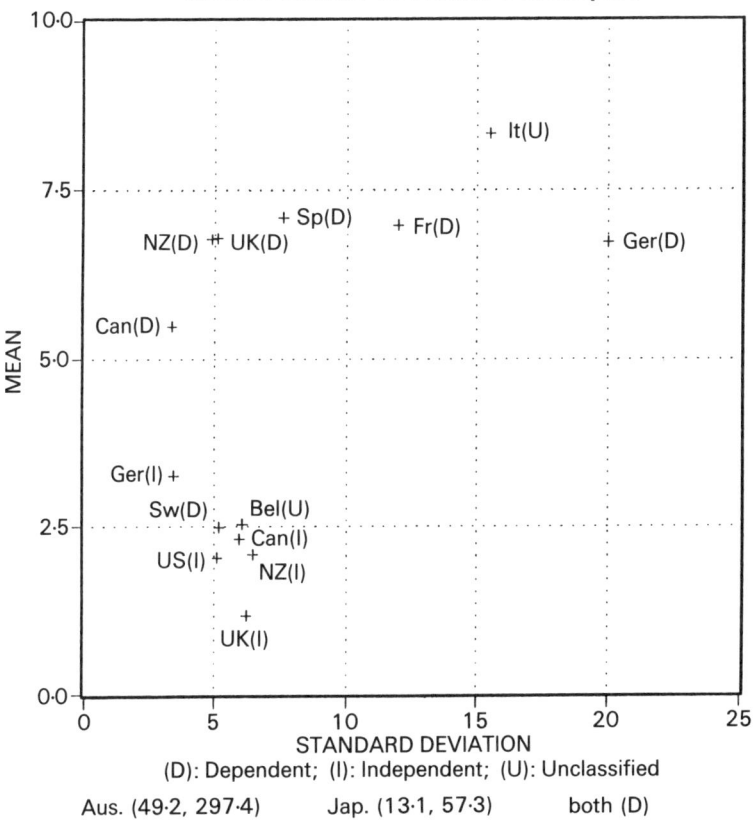

(D): Dependent; (I): Independent; (U): Unclassified

Aus. (49·2, 297·4)   Jap. (13·1, 57·3)   both (D)

The importance of using these robust measures in the present context is shown in Figure 8, which repeats the scatterplot of Figure 1 but this time uses the mean and standard deviation as measures of 'average' and 'variability'. Certain similarities are apparent, but the observations now fall into two different clusters: the 'low inflation' cluster containing the independent central banks plus Sweden and Belgium, and the 'high inflation' cluster containing all the other dependent central banks plus Italy. Discrimination is achieved by looking at mean inflation alone: using standard deviations to measure the variability of inflation adds little further discriminatory power.

As intimated above, most of the inflation series are 'contaminated' at frequent intervals by outliers, either appearing singly as 'spikes' or in groups as 'bursts' of aberrant inflation behaviour. This creates difficulties when one wishes to concentrate on the long-run inflation experience of individual countries, for short-run aberrant inflation behaviour has to be ignored. Smoothing the data is thus necessary to extract the underlying, long-run pattern from the short-run 'noise'. There are many methods of doing this, ranging from fitting a constant mean or linear trend, through computing moving averages, to estimating a trend via the technique of signal extraction. The more sophisticated the method, the more formal and specific are the assumptions that need to be made about the underlying statistical models.

Given the exploratory nature of our analysis, we wish to discover long-run patterns while making as few assumptions about the data as possible, using techniques with properties that are robust to a wide range of circumstances. Non-linear data smoothers provide a practical method of finding general smooth patterns for time-series data that are 'contaminated' with outliers, as with the inflation data analysed here.

The non-linear smoother employed in Figures 6 and 7 is that originally proposed by Tukey (1977), known as 3RSSH, twice. It is based on using repeated running medians of order 3, with additional embellishments to smooth end values (required because values before and after the sample, which are needed to compute medians, are missing) and to eradicate certain undesirable features of median smoothers: for example, running medians of order 3 have a tendency to chop off 'peaks' and 'valleys' in the data, leaving flat 'mesas' and 'dales' two observations wide. These flat segments can be smoothed by an operation known as 'splitting'.[1]

---

[1] Mills (1990, Chapter 4) provides a textbook discussion of this particular smoother and illustrates how it may be computed using only a hand calculator, although for the computations carried out for this paper, special computer algorithms were written.

References

Alesina, A. (1988): 'Macroeconomics and Politics', *NBER Macroeconomic Annual 1988*, Cambridge, Mass.: MIT Press.

Alesina, A. (1989): 'Politics and Business Cycles in Industrial Democracies', *Economic Policy*, April, pp. 55-98.

Alesina, A. and Summers, L. H. (1991): 'Central Bank Independence and Macroeconomic Performance: Some Comparative Evidence', Harvard Institute of Economic Research, Discussion Paper No. 1,496.

Bade, R. and Parkin, M. (1987): 'Central Bank Laws and Monetary Policy', University of Western Ontario, Department of Economics Discussion Paper.

Barro, R. J. and Gordon, D. B. (1983): 'A Positive Theory of Monetary Policy in a Natural Rate Model', *Journal of Political Economy*, Vol. 91, pp. 589-610.

Barro, R. J. (1986): 'Rules versus Discretion', in C. D. Campbell and W. R. Dougan (eds.), *Alternative Monetary Regimes*, Baltimore and London: Johns Hopkins University Press.

Bernholz, P. (1986): 'The Implementation and Maintenance of a Monetary Constitution', *Cato Journal*, Vol. 6, pp. 477-511.

Capie, F. H. (1986): 'Conditions in Which Very Rapid Inflation has Occurred', Carnegie-Rochester Conference Series on Public Policy, *Journal of Monetary Economics*, Vol. 24, pp. 115-68.

Capie, F. H. and Wood, G. E. (1991): 'Central Banks and Inflation: An Historical Perspective', *Central Banking*, Vol. 2, Nos. 2 and 3.

Capie, F. H., Mills, T. C. and Wood, G. E. (1992): 'Central Bank Dependence and Inflation Performance: An Exploratory Data Analysis', City University Business School, Centre for the Study of Monetary History, Discussion Paper 34.

Cukierman, A. (1992): *Central Bank Strategy, Credibility and Independence: Theory and Evidence*, Boston: MIT Press.

Friedman, M. (1960): *A Program for Monetary Stability*, New York: Fordham University Press.

Friedman, M. (1962): 'Should There be an Independent Monetary Authority?', in L. B. Yeager (ed.), *In Search of a Monetary Constitution*, Boston: Harvard University Press; reprinted 1968 in M. Friedman, *Dollars and Deficits*, Englewood Cliffs, New Jersey: Prentice-Hall.

Friedman, M. and Schwartz, A. J. (1991): 'Alternative Approaches to Analysing Economic Data', *American Economic Review*, Vol. 81, No. 1, pp. 39-49.

Grossman, H. E. (1991): 'Monetary Economics: A Review Essay', *Journal of Monetary Economics*, Vol. 28, pp. 323-46.

Hume, D. (1754): 'Of the Balance of Trade', in *Essays Moral, Political, and Literary*, reprinted e.g. 1987, Indianapolis: Liberty Press.

Masciandero, D. and Tabellini, G. (1988): 'Monetary Regimes and Fiscal Deficits: a Comparative Analysis', in A. F. Cheng (ed.), *Monetary Policy in the Pacific Basin Countries*, Dordrecht: Kluwer Academic.

Mills, T. C. (1990): *Time Series Techniques for Economists*, Cambridge: Cambridge University Press.

Mitchell, B. R. (1981): *European Historical Statistics 1750-1975*, London: Macmillan.

Mitchell, B. R. (1982): *International Historical Statistics: Africa and Asia*, London: Macmillan.

Mitchell, B. R. (1983): *International Historical Statistics: The Americas and Australasia*, London: Macmillan.

Tukey, J. W. (1977): *Exploratory Data Analysis*, Reading, Mass.: Addison-Wesley.

Williamson, J. H. and Wood, G. E. (1976): 'The British Inflation – Indigenous or Imported?', *American Economic Review*, Vol. 76, pp. 520-31.